The Incomplete Book
of
Australian Mammals

VERSES BY Ronald Strahan

PAINTINGS AND DRAWINGS BY Pamela Conder

Kangaroo Press

Ronald Strahan taught zoology in several universities before becoming Director of Sydney's Taronga Zoo, after which he was appointed Research Fellow in the Australian Museum, and later head of its National Photographic Index of Australian Wildlife, where he wrote or edited nineteen books on Australian mammals, birds, reptiles and frogs, the best known of which is the authoritative *Complete Book of Australian Mammals*. He was made a Member of the Order of Australia in 1995.

Pamela Condor is a distinguished artist, author and naturalist, who has travelled extensively studying wildlife. She has held many highly successful solo exhibitions in Australia and Europe. Her honours include the 1991 Science and Humanities Fellowship of the Museum of Victoria, the 1995 Whitely award for the Best Popular Natural History Book, and seven awards from the Wildlife Art Society of Australasia for painting, drawing and sculpture.

© Ronald Strachan (text) © Pamela Condor (illustrations) 1997

First published in Australia in 1997 by Kangaroo Press
an imprint of Simon & Schuster (Australia) Pty Limited
20 Barcoo Street, East Roseville NSW 2069

Paperback edition first published 1999

A Viacom Company
Sydney New York London Toronto Tokyo Singapore

ISBN 0 7318 0786 3

Printed in Hong Kong by South China Printing Co. Ltd

10 9 8 7 6 5 4 3 2 1

Contents

Foreword

What a wonderful thing it is that one of Australia's foremost zoologists should join hands with a leading wildlife artist to produce a book of verse and art which celebrates Australia's unique mammals. Each has spent a lifetime studying wildlife, and each brings unique skills and experience to bear on this truly joint venture. Here, their humour and eye for detail combine in a poetical tribute to Australia's native mammals.

In the early 1980s, Ronald Strahan conceived, edited and brought to publication a landmark work, *The Complete Book of Australian Mammals*. For the first time, people could see photographs of nearly all of Australia's mammals, and read of the latest findings concerning their biology. In *The Incomplete Book of Australian Mammals* the reader will find a very different work. Because it deals with a selection of Australia's mammals, it is in a sense 'incomplete'. Yet, in another way it is a more complete work, for we see our fauna through a very different, more impressionistic (even holistic) lens.

What I like most about this book is that the poems and drawings bring us close to the very essence of the animals they concern. We see the world as they might experience it.

Just how necessary it is to cultivate a love of nature in the community as a whole is brought home forcefully in the poignant poem *Thylacine*, where we learn that the species was exterminated within the lifetime of this book's author.

An empathy with nature. An understanding of the way it works. A love of natural heritage. What a gift for all Australians!

Dr Timothy Flannery
Principal Research Scientist
Australian Museum

Introduction

This little book is the work of two people who have shared the privilege of leading lives deeply involved with animals of various kinds. Both have long been fascinated by our native mammals and concerned, in their separate ways, to evoke similar feelings in others.

Pamela Conder's unique approach to depicting wildlife, based on studies of living animals, and using a variety of innovative techniques, has won her many awards.

Ronald Strahan's contribution, as the author and editor of many zoological publications has, until now, been decidedly academic. He is perhaps best known to the wider public as the editor of the standard reference on Australian mammals, The *Australian Museum Complete Book of Australian Mammals**, from which the title of this volume is derived. Until now, his skills as a versifier in matters mammalogical have been enjoyed chiefly by a rather select audience of members of the Australian Mammal Society.

The Incomplete Book of Australian Mammals is a collection of our favourite mammals, whether by reason of scientific interest, artistic appeal or simply for the fun of playing with a name. In both verse and picture we offer you an incomplete account, but one which aims to share whatever it is of the animal's essence that piques our interest, in the hope that it will not only amuse you, but arouse your curiosity.

Dear reader — whatever your age — please receive this in a sense of celebration.

Ronald Strahan and Pamela Conder

*First published by The Australian Museum and Angus & Robertson 1984. Republished as *The Mammals of Australia* by The Australian Museum and Reed Books Sydney 1995.

Koala

In the heat of the day in an average zoo,
What's a koala most likely to do?
In the fork of a tree, in a featureless heap,
It closes its eyes and endeavours to sleep.

And the visiting children and parents, they both
Say, 'Oh, what a lazy marsupial sloth!
'It's far too lethargic to romp or to toil,
'Perhaps it is drunk on the eucalypt oil.'

But that isn't fair; it's improper to mock
A creature that works to a different clock.
The schedule koalas are destined to keep
Is to deal with their business while *we* are asleep.

And, up in the treetops, throughout the long night,
They climb and they feed and make love, or they fight.
And if they took notice of me or of you,
They'd probably think *we're* a sluggardly crew.

Feathertail Glider

Picture a mammal as small as a mouse is,
Thin fold of skin from each ankle to knee,
Tail like a feather to steer it precisely,
Launching itself from the top of a tree.

Always descending, but swooping and swerving,
Dodging each obstacle found in its way:
This is the feathertail glider in action,
Putting its aerial skills on display.

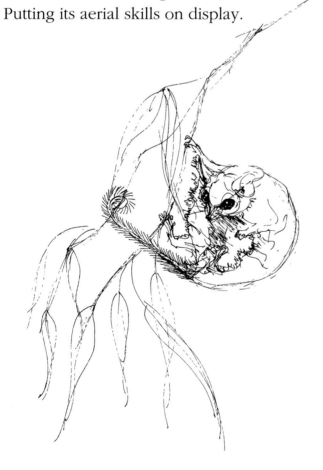

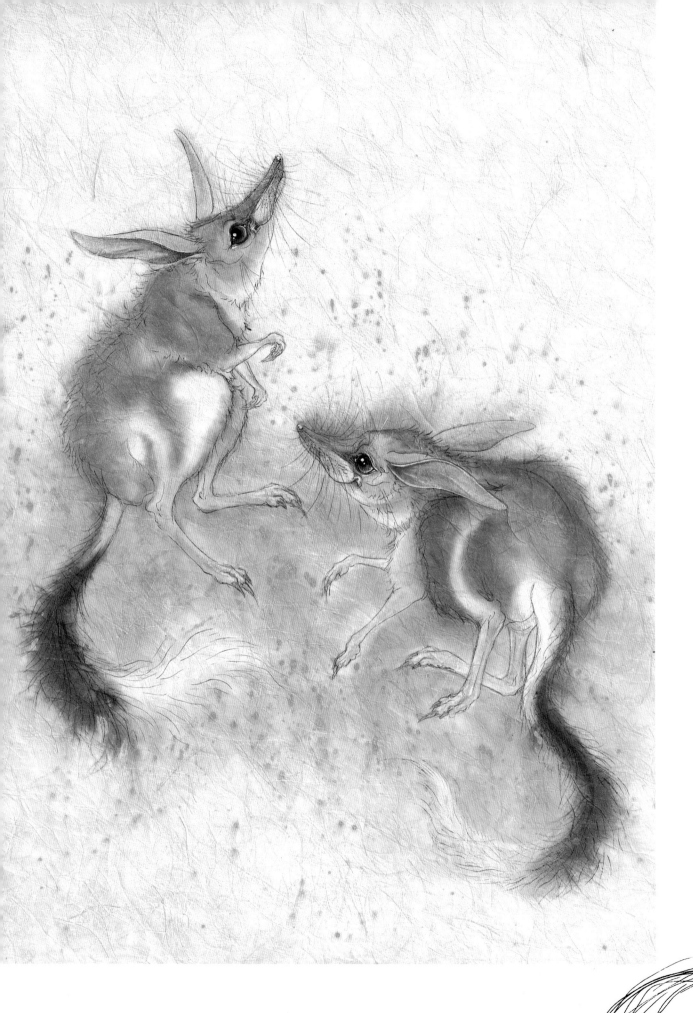

Bilby

From out of its burrow deep under the ground,
The bilby emerges with hardly a sound.
At night, in the Tanami's barren expanse,
Alone, it performs its peculiar dance.

    Dig a little here with the strong foreclaws,
    Dig a little there, then take a pause;
    Pick up a grub in the delicate snout;
    Stand up erect and sniff about.

Fur shining silvery under the moon,
It shuffles and hops to its own silent tune.
Long ears alert and its tail like a banner,
Rump bouncing high in the bandicoot manner.

    Take a little hop on the long hindfeet
    (Reasonably effectual but not quite neat);
    Run a few steps in a wobbly gait;
    Squat on the ground for a while and wait.

Not many people are given the chance
To spy on a bilby engaged in its dance;
Cats are abundant and, where the cats thrive,
Very few bilbies are still left alive.

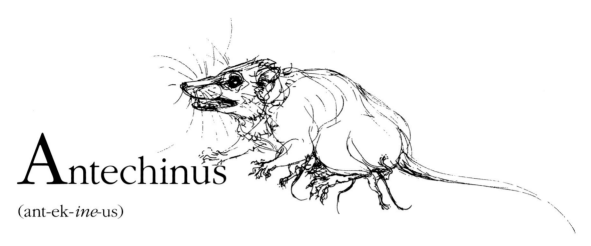

Antechinus

(ant-ek-*ine*-us)

You may sometimes hear a female antechinus crying, 'ouch!',
For although she's a marsupial, she's hardly got a pouch.
Her young hang from her nipples, which is something of a strain,
And since they hang on with their teeth, they cause a bit of pain.

A baby antechinus's existence isn't fun.
It bumps along the ground whenever mother has to run.
And father's life could not be said to be a bed of roses:
He mates when he is one year old, and then turns up his toeses.

In rating beasts I'd like to be, I find that antechinuses,
Score not a single plus and have a multitude of minuses.

Pebble-mound Mouse

Most rodents have found
That a life underground
Gives all of the shelter they need.
Their burrows provide
A safe place to hide
And to bring up their young when they breed.

But if their domain
Is the harsh gibber plain,
With ground that's as hard to dig into
As solid cement —
And one can't make a dent —
It isn't worthwhile to begin to.

So the pebble-mound mouse
Builds a sort of a house
Out of thousands of stones in a heap;
And, inside this mound
It can live *above* ground
Quite as well as the mice that dig deep.

Common Wombat

The wombat is unsociable
And not at all inclined
To any sort of fellowship
With those of its own kind.

If wombats meet each other
When foraging at night,
They grunt most impolitely
But do not stop to fight.

Each individual turns aside
And takes a new direction.
If such behaviour leads to peace,
Why bother with affection?

Tasmanian Devil

The devil makes horrible noises;
It grunts and it howls and it screams.
These blood-chilling cries
Only serve to disguise
That it isn't as fierce as it seems.

Its razor-sharp teeth are enormous;
Its mouth seems too large for its head.
But the powerful jaws
Are no danger, because
They are used to eat things that are dead.

Despite its ferocious appearance,
The devil's no more than an imp.
Although it looks tough,
This is really a bluff.
The Tasmanian devil's a wimp.

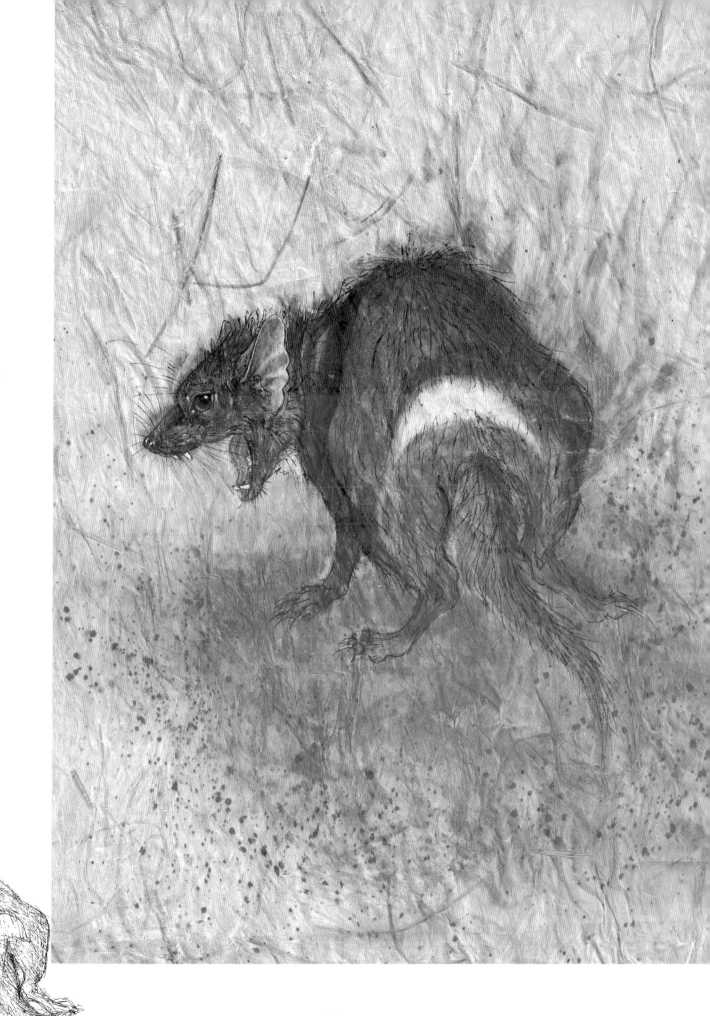

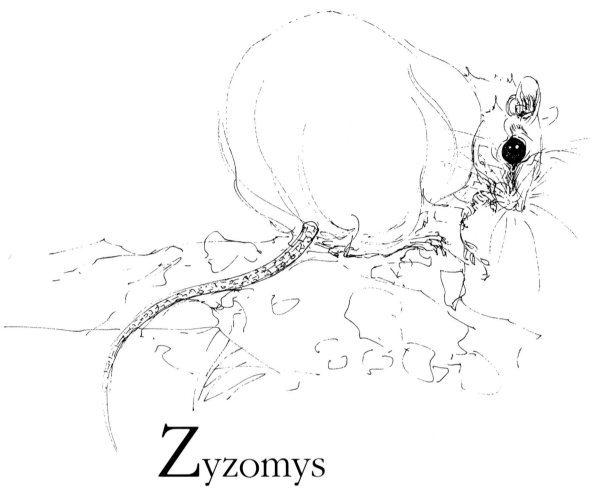

Zyzomys

(*ziz*-oh-mis)

The trouble with an animal that has a name like this is:
Should a married *Zyzomys* be called a 'zyzomissus'?
And are her female offspring each the other's 'zyzosister'?
And how do we address their dad — as 'sir' or 'zyzomister'?
A *Zyzomys* dismisses this and all related quizzes
As not at all its business: it just curls up and zizzes.

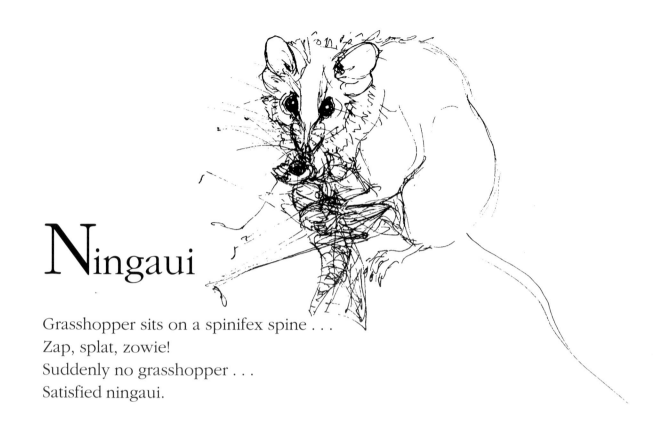

Ningaui

Grasshopper sits on a spinifex spine . . .
Zap, splat, zowie!
Suddenly no grasshopper . . .
Satisfied ningaui.

Planigale

As mammals go, a planigale
Is very, very flat,
Resembling a mouse
On which an elephant has sat.

Yellow-bellied Glider

You hear a high-pitched shriek that fades
Into a rattling cry;
A yellow-bellied glider is
Quite probably nearby.

You might, at night, perhaps take fright
And think of evil powers.
But do not fear this animal;
It feeds on sap and flowers.

Numbat

Moving at tremendous speed
Faster than the eye can follow,
Numbat's tongue picks termites up,
Flick and flick, and swallow, swallow.

Nothing more that I can say
In the form of rhyme or metre.
Numbat is essentially
A marsupial termite-eater.

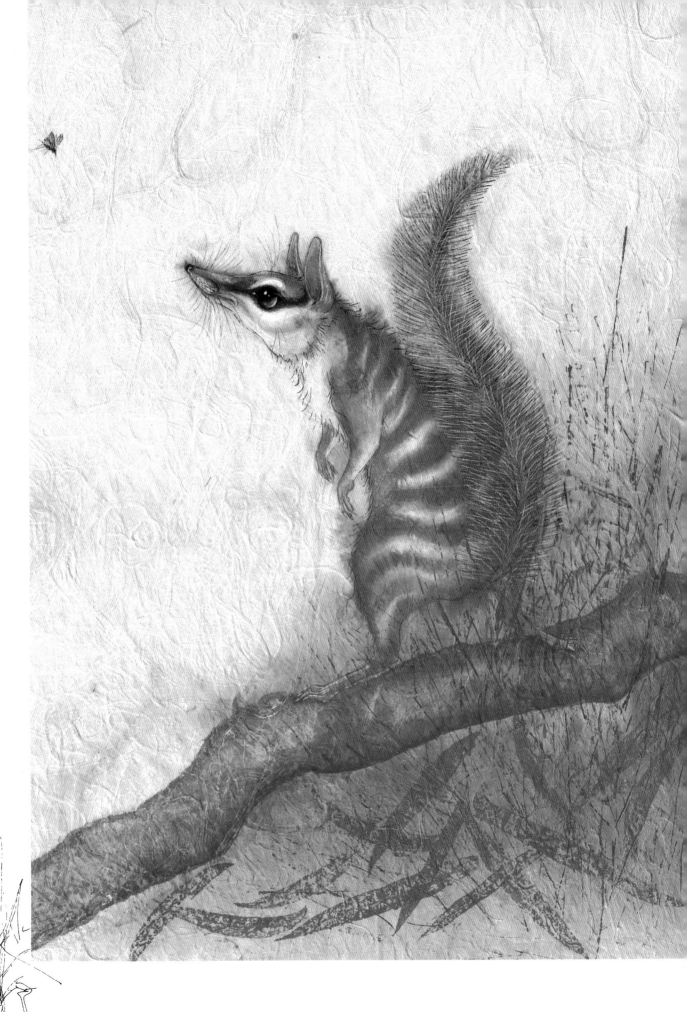

Platypus

The first *Ornithorhynchus*
Confused early thinkers.
They said, 'Oh good lord,
It's an obvious fraud!

'Somebody has stuck
The front end of a duck
(With the skill of a weaver)
To part of a beaver.

'It's no less a fake
Than the mermaids they make
From a fish and an ape —
A ridiculous jape!'

We now know it's real
Though I can't help but feel
That from tail tip to muzzle,
It still is a puzzle.

Echidna

Long beak snuffling,
Short legs shuffling,
Tachyglossus waddles on its daily quest.
Always solitary,
Hesitant and wary,
Searching for its dinner in a meat-ant nest.
Strong claws scratching,
Bent on catching
Insects that come swarming when their nest is breached;
Fast tongue flicking,
Ants are sticking
To it everywhere the probing tip has reached.
Everything alarmful
Might be harmful:
Any slight disturbances are danger signs.
Instantly reacting
Head and feet retracting,
Suddenly it turns into a ball of spines.

Striped Possum

If you see a furry creature,
Brightly striped in white and black,
Have no fear that it will eat yer;
It's unlikely to attack.

What its colour pattern's telling,
To a predator that thinks,
Is that it is nasty-smelling;
Very possibly it stinks.

Skunks use smell in their defences.
To a somewhat less extent,
Dactylopsila offends us
With its own unpleasant scent.

If, in search of native fauna,
You should come across striped possums,
Leave them in their private corner,
And their world of bugs and blossoms.

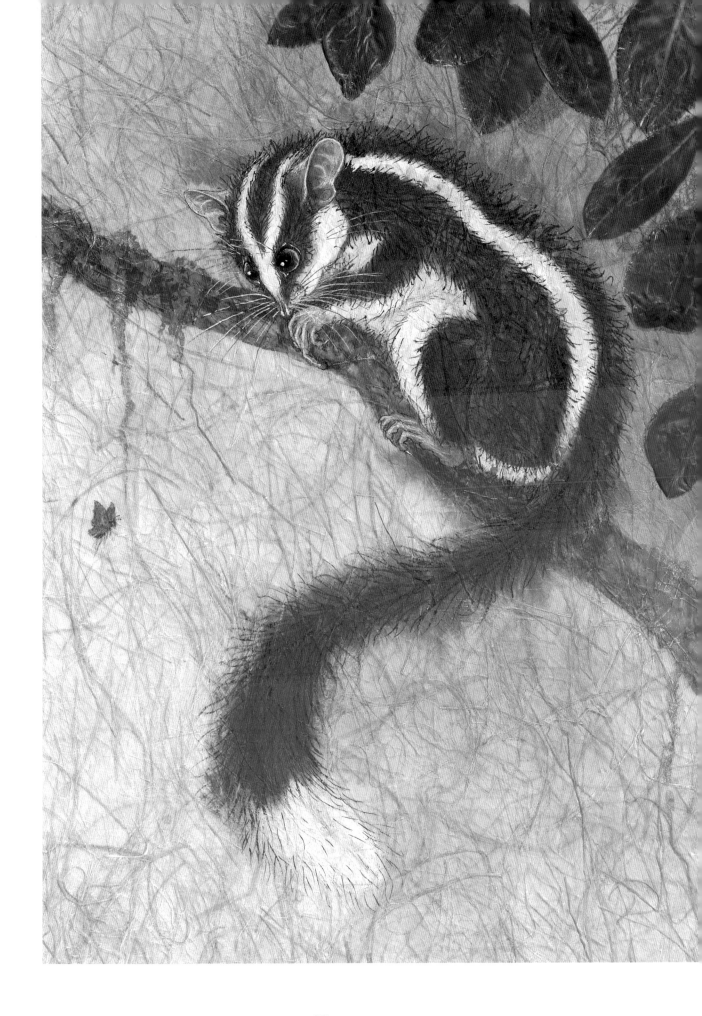

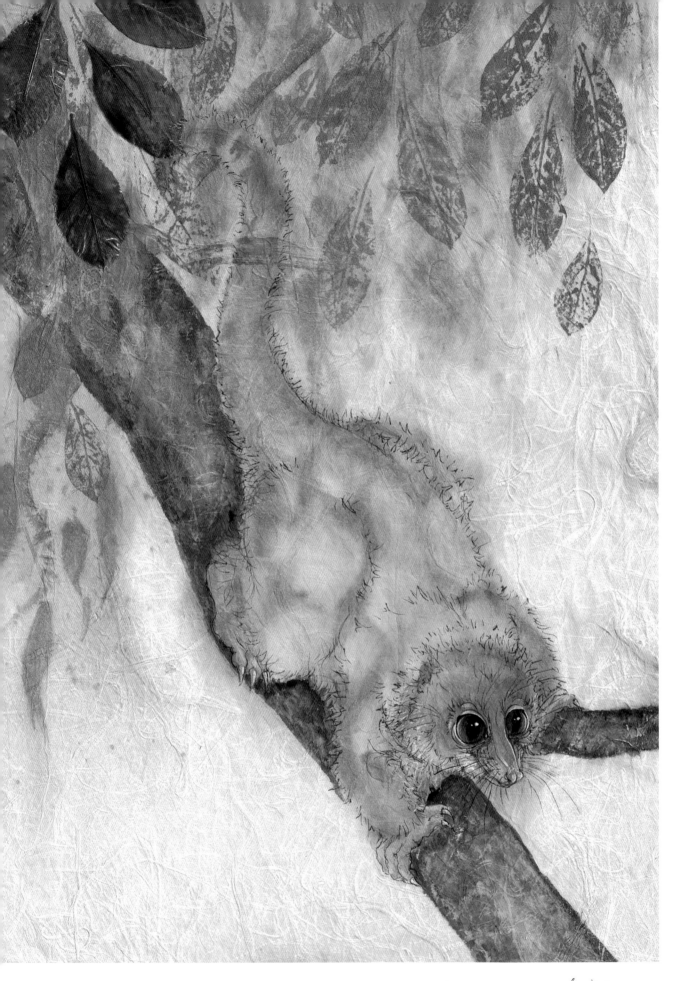

Cuscus

Flattish face with tiny ears,
Large round eyes that peer ahead,
Cuscuses resemble monkeys
(So the first explorers said).

Actually, they're largish possums,
Living in the tops of trees,
Moving slowly through the forest
With a strangely fluid ease.

Hands and feet grip most securely
And, if these should ever fail,
Cuscuses support their bodies
With a strong prehensile tail.

'Slow but sure' their way of life is
(Quite unlike a monkey's spryness).
Cuscuses are rather sloth-like
In their sluggishness and shyness.

Tree Kangaroo

Some fifty million years ago, a possum looked around
And wondered if it might do better living on the ground.

Descending from the trees, it found, upon the forest floor,
Abundant food but, when it felt a need for somewhat more,
It had to move onto the plains, and this was rather stressful,
For enemies abounded, but the possum was successful.

It grew enormous hindlegs in a manner rather new,
Invented hopping and became a little kangaroo.
And, from this little one, a host of bigger ones evolved.
One might have thought the problems had been very neatly solved.

But then one kangaroo, despite its life of peace and ease,
Decided to investigate a life back in the trees.
It wasn't very agile but it found a rough solution:
By utterly reversing all its previous evolution.

Hindquarters shrank, forequarters grew, the tail just limply dangled;
A very clumsy compromise, no matter how new-fangled.
And that, my dear, is how we came to have tree kangaroos.
No further explanation; all I do is give the news.

Nabarlek

Over there you can see
If you carefully check,
On the edge of the scree
Is a fine nabarlek.

Just the glimpse of an ear
And the hint of its shoulder . . .
No longer, I fear;
It bounced off that boulder.

Did you notice it then
Or at least get a peep
In the brief moment when
It was making a leap?

Can you see where it darted?
It's coming our way!
Or was 'til it started
That last ricochet.

And off it goes, bounding
From cliff face to cleft
With skill that's astounding:
No trace of it left.

No mad mountaineer
Was ever so reckless.
I'm sorry, my friend,
That you're still nabarlekless.

Red Kangaroo

Through mulga and mallee, with soft, thudding sound,
The red kangaroo moves in bound after bound
On the tips of its toes in a firm, steady pace
That covers the country with effortless grace.

Since pasture is scanty and waterholes few
In the harsh, arid home of the red kangaroo,
It must travel great distances, never once stopping,
But endlessly, patiently, hopping and hopping.

Phascogale

Although phascogales
Have bottle-brush tails,
We simply don't know
Why this should be so.
I have to confess
It's anyone's guess.

How well would they fare
If the brush wasn't there?

Fat-tailed Dunnart

The fat-tailed dunnart fiercely preys
On insects, spiders, centipedes,
And, in the summer, finds that these
Provide more tucker than it needs.

The extra food is stored away
As fat within the dunnart's tail,
And there it serves as a reserve
If food supply begins to fail.

So, when the end of winter comes —
And if the season's been unkind —
Its name is not appropriate:
A *thin*-tailed dunnart's what we find.

Ghost Bat

Out of its cave when the daylight has ended
Comes a most horrible pale apparition,
Silently swooping on slow wings extended,
Bent on its nocturnal predatory mission.

Birds of the night, even little bats flying,
Frogs or small mammals in perilous places,
Whether they sense it or not, are defying
Death in the ghost bat's swift final embraces.

Quolls

When talking of marsupials,
I always tell my pupials
That dasyurids, on the whole, are very much the same.
One has to be a quibbler
To judge just how a dibbler
Is different from a dunnart: it's a very tricky game.

But quolls are recognisable
In being rather sizeable
And all the members of the group to which they are allotted
Are *very* easily defined;
If you will only keep in mind
That quolls are those that have a fur that's quite distinctly spotted.

Honey Possum

To find the rather strange and quite elusive honey possums,
You must search among the banksias and other heathland blossoms
Of southern West Australia, because these are what they need
To provide supplies of nectar upon which these possums feed.

The mouse-sized honey possum is extremely specialised:
Its long and brush-tipped tongue is very beautifully devised
To dip into a banksia flower, remove its hidden store
Of nectar and of pollen, and move on to take some more.

Some pollen sticks to hairs upon its elongated snout
And, as it moves from bloom to bloom, the pollen's spread about.
So, if you make comparisons, it isn't hard to see
The honey possum as a sort of big marsupial bee.

Flying-fox

Hanging by their toes and wrapped securely in their wings,
Flying-foxes seem to be extraordinary things —
Like some blackish fruits a tree has suddenly produced —
But look again more closely at these bats within their roost.
Most of them are moving and engaged in competition,
Squabbling and squeaking as they jostle for position.
Some are very busy at what humans would call wooing,
Others tend their babies but, no matter what they're doing,
All look rather awkward in their actions through the day.
Living upside down is not a very easy way.
Transformation comes with the beginning of the night:
Flying-foxes leave the trees in thousands to take flight.
Spreading wings, they circle up and we become aware
That they are strangely beautiful when they are in the air.

Marsupial Mole

The marsupial mole
Doesn't live in a hole
Or a burrow or funnel
Or underground tunnel.

It swims through the sands
With its shovel-like hands
And the sand, as it's mined,
Simply falls in behind.

So nobody knows
How it comes or it goes
Or where it has been,
Which is why it's not seen.

Water-rat

I live beside a waterhole,
An inland river or a creek;
My upper fur is dark and dense
And waterproof and very sleek.
My belly and my chest display
A hue of yellow or of gold,
So millions of my relatives
Were trapped and then their skins were sold
To make smart coats for you and yours
Upon the supposition that
Fur's better on a human than
An unrespected water rat.

Who cares what happens to a rat?
The word's enough to damn one's soul.
You could have named us otherwise:
Perhaps 'Australian water vole'.
But *rat*'s the name *you* gave to us!
Before your people came along,
The first Australians knew us well
As palarale or tularong.

Koala, bilby, potoroo,
Are creatures you appreciate.
I wonder if, with names like theirs,
We might have had a better fate.

Elephant Seal

The rubbery, blubbery elephant seal
(It's the bull I'm referring to now)
Is the clumsiest beast ever seen on the land
(The same isn't true of the cow).

Its three tonnes of meat are too much for its feet
They're unable to handle the weight.
So it wriggles and squirms in the manner of worms;
It has a ridiculous gait.

And it has to be said that the shape of its head
Is peculiar. The nose, as it grows,
Becomes a great lump in the form of a trumpet
Through which it makes hoots when it blows.

It never was planned for life on the land;
It comes ashore only for breeding
And spends its time fighting by bashing and biting
Until it is battered and bleeding.

But, back in the ocean, its elegant motion
Puts fishes and dolphins to shame.
Apart from its face, it's a creature of grace,
Deserving of proper acclaim.

What's true of these seals maybe also reveals
A thought that applies to us, too.
Let's all be assessed by the things we do best,
Not those we can *only just* do.

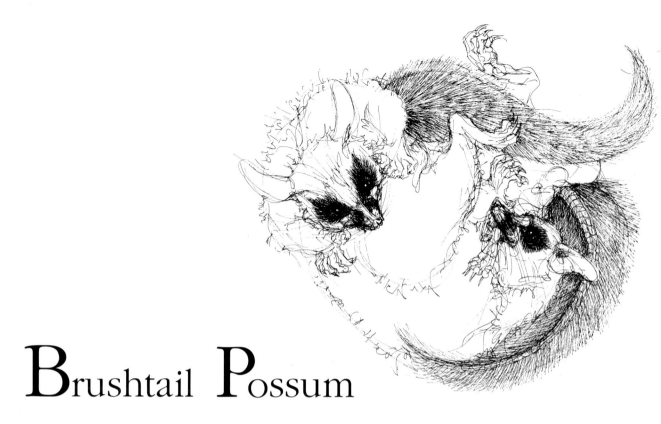

Brushtail Possum

A brushtail possum made a nest above my bedroom ceiling.
At first I thought this showed a very pleasant fellow-feeling:
Instead of nesting in a tree and utterly aloof,
He'd chosen, in a friendly way, to live beneath my roof.

But then some other possums thought that they would move in too,
To which the first objected and the air at night was blue
With bumps and thumps and hisses, growls and awful throaty gagging,
And where those possum combats raged, my ceiling started sagging.

'Til softened up by possum pee, one memorable night,
A patch gave way and, still engaged in bitter, snarling fight,
Two possums landed on my bed, then charged around the room
(Their panic was no less than mine, I'm sure I must assume.)

I threw the window open wide: they fled I know not where,
Nor, honestly, I must admit, am I prepared to care
Where either of them settled down; for soon my eaves and roof
Were treated to ensure they were securely possum-proof.
And, as to our relationship, I say to possums, 'Please
Refrain from living in my house and I won't nest in trees'.

Thylacine

I wish, just once, that I had been
Around to see a thylacine.
I'm quite familiar with its looks
From illustrations in old books,
Stuffed specimens in museum cases,
Skeletons in various places,
Photographs of hunters posed
With carcases that they supposed
Showed hunting thylacines was fun
And credit to the snare and gun.
Some jerky movie shots survive
To show some in a cage, alive.

I might have seen one if I'd tried:
I was a boy when the last one died.

Notes

The **Koala** is a large, tree-dwelling animal which, like most other marsupials, sleeps during the day. However, because it does not use a den or make a nest, it can be *seen* when it is sleeping and this is why it has the reputation of being unusually inactive. The popular idea that it is 'drugged' on oil in the eucalyptus leaves that it eats is quite incorrect: eucalyptus oil has no such effect.

Weighing about 12 grams, the **Feathertail Glider** is by far the smallest of the gliding possums. Long stiff hairs projecting on either side of the tail create a featherlike structure that contributes to steering in flight. It feeds on nectar, pollen and small insects.

The rare and endangered **Bilby** resembles bandicoots but differs from them in having rabbit-like ears, long silky fur, and a brush-tipped tail. During the day, it sleeps in a deep burrow. At night, it digs in the sand for burrowing insects and succulent parts of plants. When moving slowly, it has a peculiar gait, between a hop and a walk. Sentimentally, I think of it as a dance — perhaps a square dance.

The genus ***Antechinus*** (ant-ek-*ine*-us) includes eight Australian species that are somewhat ratlike in appearance but range from about the size of a house mouse to about four times its weight. They feed on insects and most live on the forest floor, although some are agile climbers. The rudimentary pouch of the female does not enclose the developing young, which simply dangle from her teats. Males mate when about one year old and die shortly after.

There are three species of **pebble-mound mice**, all from stony deserts. Over the course of many generations, a local population of pebble-mound mice builds up a pile of small stones to several metres in diameter. Individual mice can transport stones up to a quarter of their own weight, carrying them between their forepaws and chin.

The **Common Wombat** inhabits forests and spends the day in an extensive burrow. At night, it moves into open areas or forest edges to graze. The home ranges of neighbouring wombats often overlap but, if two animals find themselves approaching each other, they seldom act aggressively. They usually avoid each other.

The **Tasmanian Devil** has a head that seems too large for its body, with wide-gaping jaws and large teeth. Although it takes some small prey, it is mainly a scavenger, able to eat the entire body of a kangaroo or sheep, including the skull. Unlike the distantly related thylacine ('Tasmanian tiger'), it remains quite common.

Five species of rock-rats comprise the genus **Zyzomys** (*ziz*-oh-mis). All live in rocky country in the northern half of Australia and feed mostly on seeds. The scientist who named the genus in 1909 did not explain why he had done so. He could, however, be reasonably sure that *Zyzomys* would be the last in any alphabetical list.

Three species of very small marsupials (less than ten grams) form the genus **Ningaui** (nin-*gow*-ee). They feed mainly upon insects, including grasshoppers not much smaller than themselves. This can involve a short, fierce struggle.

Planigales (*plan*-ee-gales) comprise four species of the genus *Planigale* (plan-ee-*gah*-lay), all of which are very small (some less than five grams) and have notably flattened heads. These marsupials are able to scuttle into narrow crevices or soil cracks, with their legs extended outwards from the body, somewhat like a spider. They feed mainly on insects.

The **Yellow-bellied Glider** is a largish possum that is able to glide through the air on folds of skin extending from the wrists to the ankles. It feeds on flowers and on sap that it obtains by biting into to the trunks of smooth-barked eucalypt trees. Its blood-curdling call is a territorial advertisement addressed to other members of its species.

The beautiful **Numbat**, once spread over much of southern Australia, is now endangered and restricted to a small area of wandoo forest in south-western Australia and, even there, it is threatened by the fox. It is unusual among marsupials in being active by day. It feeds exclusively on termites (white ants), which it picks up, like an echidna, on its long, sticky, fast-moving tongue.

The **Platypus** is the only species of the genus *Ornithorhynchus* (orn-ith-oh-*rink*-us), which means 'bird-snout'. It is so unlike any other mammal that the first specimens to reach Europe were regarded as fakes. The platypus is unusual in many respects, such as hatching its young from eggs, production of milk in the absence of teats or nipples, presence of a poison gland and spur on the hind legs of males, and possession of an electrical sense in the beak. There is still much to learn about this creature.

The widely-distributed **Echidna** (ee-*kid*-nah), like the platypus, is an egg-layer. Sharp spines cover its back and sides. It feeds on ants, particularly meat-ants, picked up on its long, sticky tongue in the same way that a numbat eats termites. Intensely nervous, it reacts to any disturbance by 'freezing' and, if threatened, it either rolls into a ball or digs itself into the ground.

One species of **Striped Possum** occurs in Australia. Others occur in New Guinea. When handled, they give off an unpleasant odour but this is much less offensive than that of the similarly coloured skunk of North America. A peculiar feature of striped possums is the very long fourth finger, used to extract beetle larvae that burrow in the branches of trees.

There are many different **cuscuses** in the New Guinea region but only two in Australia, both from the rainforests of North Queensland. Cuscuses, which feed mainly on leaves and blossoms, are very deliberate climbers, moving through the forest canopy with a slow, gliding motion. Their rather flat faces are somewhat monkey-like but any resemblance ends there.

Most **tree kangaroos** are found in the New Guinea region but two occur in North Queensland. They are improbable creatures. Typical kangaroos evolved from possum-like marsupials by development of large hind legs, used in a hopping gait. Tree-kangaroos, which feed mostly on the leaves of rainforest trees, evolved from ground-dwelling kangaroos by reversing this process, shortening the hind feet and enlarging the fore legs. They are awkward but effective climbers.

The **Nabarlek** (*nah*-bar-lek) is one of the smallest of the rock-wallabies, weighing about 1.5 kilograms. It is extremely agile on cliffs and rock-faces and can be thought of, like other rock-wallabies, as a 'marsupial mountain-goat'.

The largest member of its family, the **Red Kangaroo** extends further into the deserts than any other kangaroo. It moves from one area of food and water to another in a graceful hopping motion that can be maintained for hours at a time. Interestingly, a hopping kangaroo expends much less energy than a four-legged animal of the same size, moving at the same speed.

Phascogales (*fas*-koh-gales), which are related to antechinuses, are very agile climbers that often leap several metres from one branch to another. They feed mainly on insects and spiders. Like antechinuses, males mate when about one year old and die shortly after.

About 20 species of dunnarts comprise the species *Sminthopsis* (sminth-<u>op</u>-sis), which means 'mouse-like' and refers to their size and shape. They are agile, ground-dwelling marsupials that prey upon large insects and small reptiles. The **Fat-tailed Dunnart** and several others store fat in the tail, which becomes carrot-shaped when food is plentiful. When food is scarce, the fat provides a reserve of food.

The bats of the world fall into two distinct groups. The megabats (flying-foxes and fruit bats) are mostly large, feed on fruits or nectar, and navigate by sight. The much more numerous microbats are mostly small, feed on insects, have tiny eyes, and navigate by echolocation. The **Ghost Bat**, by far the largest of the microbats, is unusual in combining good vision with echolocation. It is a very efficient predator on other vertebrate animals.

Dasyurids (daz-ee-*yue*-rids) comprise a large group of flesh-eating marsupials ranging in size from the Tasmanian Devil to tiny ningauis and planigales. **Quolls** are middle-sized dasyurids and are excellent climbers. They prey upon small mammals and birds. Apart from one species of cuscus, they are the only Australian mammals with spotted fur.

The tiny **Honey Possum** is so specialised for a diet of nectar and pollen that its teeth are reduced to slender, blunt pegs. It is restricted to the heathland of south-western Australia, probably because this is the only region where at least some flowers are in bloom throughout the year. Like a bee, the honey possum pays for its food by transferring pollen from one flower to another.

There are some 70 species of **flying-foxes**, seven of which occur in Australia. Largest of the living bats, flying-foxes have a rather doglike head, with large eyes. During the day, they roost in trees, often in colonies of several hundred thousand individuals. At night, they fly out from the roost, using well-developed senses of sight and smell, in search of forest fruits and blossoms — or orchards.

The verse about the **Marsupial Mole** summarises most of our knowledge of this strange animal. It is blind, it lacks external ears and its tail is a short stump. It is seldom seen, except after heavy rains have saturated the sand in which it spends its life.

The **Water-rat** is a rodent, but only distantly related to the 'true' rats. It swims with its webbed hind feet and feeds on a wide range of smaller aquatic animals: it could be thought of as the Australian equivalent of water voles, or even otters. It was once hunted extensively for its dense, waterproof fur and — due also to destruction of much of its habitat — it is far less common than it was a century or so ago.

The **Southern Elephant Seal** is by far the largest of seals of the Southern Hemisphere. Mature males, which are ten times the weight of females, have a proboscis-like structure that is associated with their roaring cries. When they come ashore to breed, males are extremely aggressive towards each other in defence of their harems of female seals. They move with great difficulty on the land, but are elegant swimmers.

The **Brushtail Possum** lives in trees and feeds mainly on leaves, blossoms and fruits. Because it often nests in the roofs of suburban houses, it is probably the most familiar of Australian marsupials — and sometimes the most unpopular. The incident related in the verse is true except that the possums fell into my daughter's bedroom, not mine.

The story of the **Thylacine** (*thigh*-lah-seen), a wolflike marsupial also called the Tasmanian Tiger, is a sad one. Because it was thought to prey upon sheep, it was persecuted by settlers and rapidly became rare. The last individual of which we have definite knowledge died in a scruffy zoo in Hobart in 1936, the year in which the Tasmanian government eventually declared it to be a totally protected species.